LIFE PICTURE PUZZLE

WELCOME TO LIFE'S NINTH

PICTURE PUZZLE BOOK

Having taken journeys across America and celebrated the traditions of the winter holidays in earlier Picture Puzzle book themes, we wondered if we (and you) could play with something completely different this time out. Wouldn't it be fun, we asked ourselves, to set our mini-mysteries against the backdrops of some of the greatest mysteries of all time? Imagine a volume in which our intrepid legion of puzzlers is joined and inspired by the likes of Sherlock Holmes, Hercule Poirot, Miss Marple, and the Thin Man. So we went to Tinseltown and came back with a trove of images from famous and not-so-famous movies and TV shows—thrillers, police procedurals, noir classics, satires, and sitcoms. It turns out that filmed mysteries and picture puzzles are made for each other, and our photo editors were able to supply our crazed puzzle master with an abundance of images that were perfect for tinkering. Also: Because many favorite stars of yesterday and today have portrayed the great detectives (and some of the great villains) down through the years, this new book is not simply another exciting trip for our dedicated puzzlers, it's a happy stroll down memory lane.

Everything you loved about our earlier books is still here. Our Novice section sets an easy pace so you can ramp up your skills as you go. Our Master and Expert sections incrementally add to the challenge, and when you tackle our Genius puzzles, you'll be a certified puzzle master yourself. Plus, as you see just below, we've invented a whole new kind of puzzle—the WHODUNIT—which unfolds in more ways than one, changing constantly as it moves through three chapters to a surprising conclusion. We think you'll love it. If you don't, well . . . we're mystified!

[OUR CUT-UP PUZZLES: EASY AS 1-2-3]

We snipped a photo into four or six pieces. Then we rearranged the pieces and numbered them.

Your mission: Beneath each cut-up puzzle, write the number of the piece in the box where it belongs.

Check the answer key at the back of the book to see what the reassembled image looks like.

And Introducing LIFE's WHODUNIT Puzzles

Since we were trying to create a new kind of Picture Puzzle book, we sought to add a brand-new type of puzzle. We call it the WHODUNIT, and there are two of them awaiting you. Not only do you get to find all the sneaky changes we put in our regular puzzles, but by following the action over six pages and three chapters, you also get to identify and perhaps solve an additional crime. So there are several small changes, then a big one. The WHODUNIT: an entirely new kind of picture puzzle for your enjoyment.

[HOW TO PLAY THE PUZZLES]

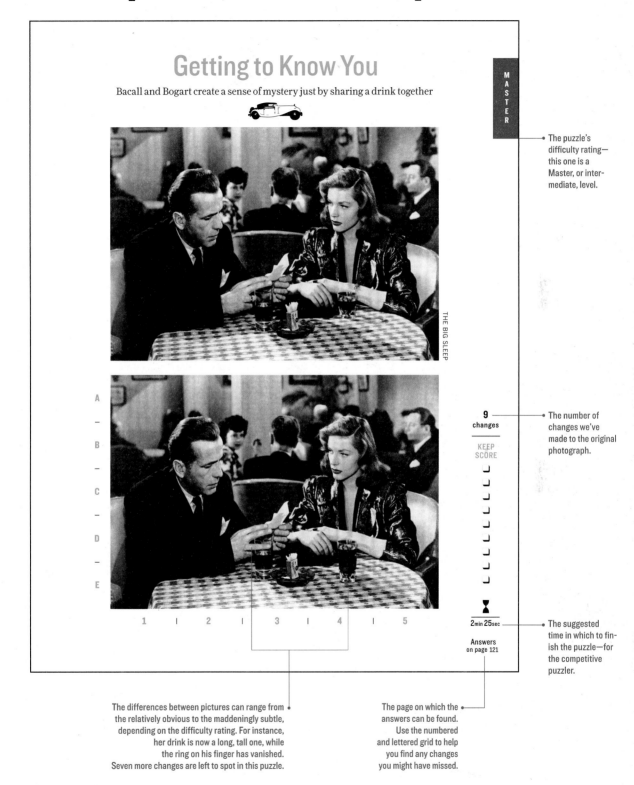

Getting to Know You

Bacall and Bogart create a sense of mystery just by sharing a drink together

MASTER

• The puzzle's difficulty rating—this one is a Master, or intermediate, level.

THE BIG SLEEP

9
changes

KEEP SCORE

2min 25sec

Answers on page 121

• The number of changes we've made to the original photograph.

• The suggested time in which to finish the puzzle—for the competitive puzzler.

The differences between pictures can range from the relatively obvious to the maddeningly subtle, depending on the difficulty rating. For instance, her drink is now a long, tall one, while the ring on his finger has vanished. Seven more changes are left to spot in this puzzle.

The page on which the answers can be found. Use the numbered and lettered grid to help you find any changes you might have missed.

LIFE PICTURE PUZZLE

Puzzle Master Michael Roseman
Editor Robert Sullivan
Director of Photography Barbara Baker Burrows
Deputy Picture Editor Christina Lieberman
Copy Barbara Gogan (Chief), Danielle Dowling

LIFE Puzzle Books
Managing Editor Bill Shapiro

LIFE Books
President Andrew Blau
Business Manager Roger Adler
Business Development Manager Jeff Burak

Editorial Operations
Richard K. Prue (Director), Brian Fellows (Manager), Keith Aurelio, Charlotte Coco,
John Goodman, Kevin Hart, Norma Jones, Mert Kerimoglu, Rosalie Khan, Patricia Koh,
Marco Lau, Brian Mai, Po Fung Ng, Lorenzo Pace, Rudi Papiri, Robert Pizaro, Barry Pribula,
Clara Renauro, Donald Schaedtler, Hia Tan, Vaune Trachtman, David Weiner

Time Inc. Home Entertainment
Publisher Richard Fraiman
General Manager Steven Sandonato
Executive Director, Marketing Services Carol Pittard
Director, Retail & Special Sales Tom Mifsud
Director, New Product Development Peter Harper
Assistant Director, Bookazine Marketing Laura Adam
Assistant Director, Brand Marketing Joy Butts
Associate Counsel Helen Wan
Book Production Manager Suzanne Janso
Design & Prepress Manager Anne-Michelle Gallero
Brand Manager Roshni Patel

Special thanks to Christine Austin, Glenn Buonocore, Jim Childs, Susan Chodakiewicz,
Rose Cirrincione, Jacqueline Fitzgerald, Lauren Hall, Jennifer Jacobs, Brynn Joyce,
Mona Li, Robert Marasco, Amy Migliaccio, Brooke Reger, Dave Rozzelle, Ilene Schreider,
Adriana Tierno, Alex Voznesenskiy, Sydney Webber, Jonathan White

PUBLISHED BY

LIFE Books

Vol. 9, No. 9 • October 9, 2009

Copyright 2009
Time Inc.
1271 Avenue of the Americas
New York, NY 10020

We welcome your comments and suggestions about LIFE Books. Please write to us at:
LIFE Books
Attention: Book Editors
PO Box 11016
Des Moines, IA 50336-1016

If you would like to order any of our hardcover Collector's Edition books, please call us at 1-800-327-6388
(Monday through Friday, 7 a.m. to 8 p.m., or Saturday, 7 a.m. to 6 p.m. Central Time).

COVER: CHROMACOME/GETTY

READY, SET,

GO!

CONTENTS

NOVICE

[
These puzzles are for everyone:
rookies and veterans,
young and old. Start here, and
sharpen your skills.
]

Shedding Light on the Case

Once a year, even detectives get to blow out a candle and make a wish

HOMICIDE: LIFE ON THE STREET/NBC

8 changes

KEEP SCORE

☐
☐
☐
☐
☐
☐
☐
☐

⏳

2min 40sec

Answers on page 121

Their Job Is Murder

They'll see that justice is done

CSI/ROBERT VOETS/CBS/GETTY

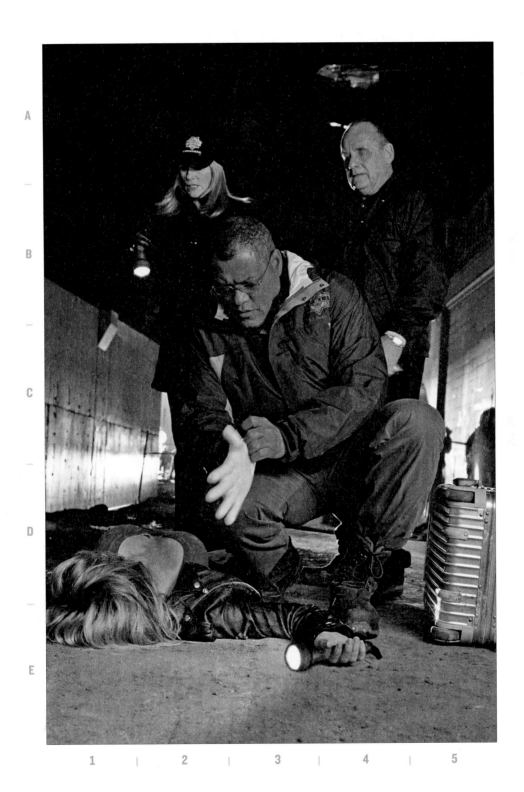

8
changes

KEEP
SCORE

❏
❏
❏
❏
❏
❏
❏
❏

⧗

2min 15sec

Answers
on page 121

Masonic Rituals

Justice may be blind, but Perry has twenty–twenty vision

PERRY MASON

9
changes

⧗
2min 40sec

Answers
on page 121

KEEP SCORE ★ ❑ ❑ ❑ ❑ ❑ ❑ ❑ ❑ ❑

Falling Dominoes

Break the kid to break the case, or watch the case break them

A
B
C
D
E

1   2   3   4   5

9
changes

⧗
2min 35sec

Answers
on page 121

KEEP SCORE ★ ☐ ☐ ☐ ☐ ☐ ☐ ☐ ☐ ☐

This Is the City

The puzzle you are about to solve is true.
Only the details have been changed to entertain the reader.

A
—
B
—
C
—
D
—
E

1   2   3   4   5

7
changes

⧗

2min 10sec

Answers
on page 121

KEEP SCORE ★ ✓✓✓☐☐☐☐

Whose Charade Is It?

He knows that she knows, but she doesn't know,
and she knows that he knows, but he doesn't know

A — B — C — D — E

1   2   3   4   5

6
changes

⧗
1min **10**sec

Answers
on page 121

KEEP SCORE ★ ❏ ❏ ❏ ❏ ❏ ❏

Five Birds of a Feather . . .

. . . and one picture that doesn't fly

1

2

3

4

5

6

0min 45sec

Answer
on page 121

THE BIRDS/UNIVERSAL STUDIO

Ectoplasmic Mischief

Ghost hunters should have no trouble divining which is different

1

2

3

4

5

6

TOPPER TAKES A TRIP

0min 55sec

Answer
on page 121

Lunge, Parry, Thrust

Never mistake Miss Marple for your average little old lady

MURDER AHOY

A

B

C

D

E

1   2   3   4   5

7
changes

KEEP
SCORE

❏
❏
❏
❏
❏
❏
❏

⧗

1min 55sec

Answers
on page 121

You're Pretty as a Picture, Laura

Both the detective and the so-called victim
have just received the surprise of their lives

LAURA/20TH CENTURY FOX/JOHN SPRINGER COLLECTION/BETTMANN/CORBIS

A
–
B
–
C
–
D
–
E

1 | 2 | 3 | 4 | 5

8
changes

⧗

3min 20sec

Answers
on page 121

KEEP SCORE ★ ❏ ❏ ❏ ❏ ❏ ❏ ❏ ❏

Lady Be Good

A criminal investigator is always supposed to be wary of rosy scenarios

CSI//ROBERT VOETS/CBS/GETTY

7
changes

KEEP
SCORE

A

B

C

D

1min 45sec

E

Answers
on page 122

1   2   3   4   5

Service for Two

His Frankenstein days far behind him, Boris, in his twilight, enjoys some tea

THE TERROR

6
changes

KEEP
SCORE

❑
❑
❑
❑
❑
❑

⧗

2min 10sec

Answers
on page 122

A
B
C
D
E

1   2   3   4   5

Disappearing Act

Houdini's got nothing on us

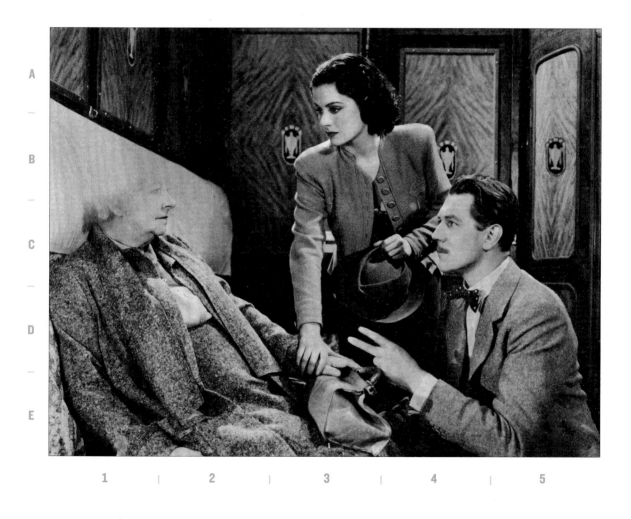

A
—
B
—
C
—
D
—
E

1   2   3   4   5

8
changes

⧗
3min 20sec

Answers
on page 122

KEEP SCORE ★ ❑ ❑ ❑ ❑ ❑ ❑ ❑ ❑

Fiddling About

This time we're not just stringing you along

A

B

C

D

E

1 | 2 | 3 | 4 | 5

8
changes

KEEP
SCORE

❑
❑
❑
❑
❑
❑
❑
❑

⏳
2min 35sec

Answers
on page 122

High Society

When the rich and famous fall, they fall hard

TWO MRS. GRENVILLES/NBC

A
—
B
—
C
—
D
—
E

1 | 2 | 3 | 4 | 5

7
changes

⧗
2min 35sec

Answers
on page 122

KEEP SCORE ★ ☐ ☐ ☐ ☐ ☐ ☐ ☐

Truth Seeker

Sometimes the search for justice doesn't end with the trial

THE FUGITIVE/BETTMANN/CORBIS

1 | 2 | 3 | 4 | 5

9
changes
___

KEEP
SCORE

❏
❏
❏
❏
❏
❏
❏
❏
❏

⧗
___
1min 55sec

Answers
on page 122

Band Practice

This ensemble has a Bogie man

10 changes

⧗

3min 35sec

Answers on page 122

KEEP SCORE ★ ☐ ☐ ☐ ☐ ☐ ☐ ☐ ☐ ☐ ☐

A Dogged Investigation

Put the pooch in a proper picture

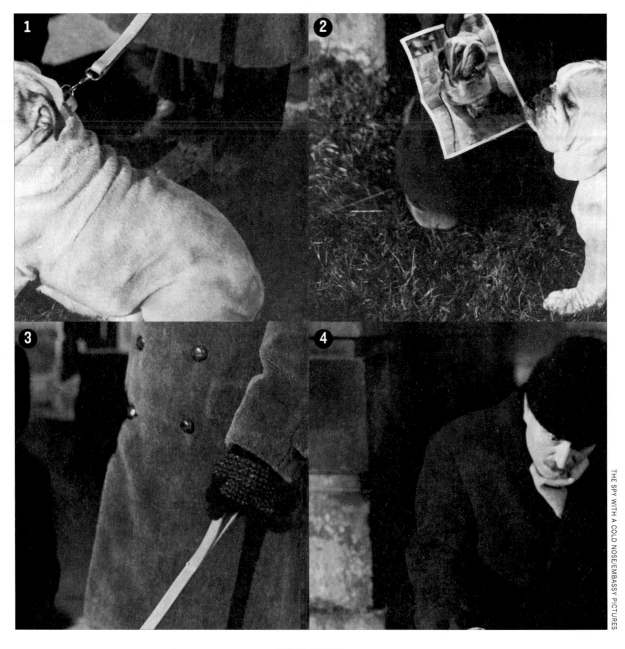

THE SPY WITH A COLD NOSE/EMBASSY PICTURES

0min 35sec

Answer
on page 122

KEEP SCORE

9
changes

KEEP
SCORE

❏
❏
❏
❏
❏
❏
❏
❏
❏

⧗
3min 55sec

Answers
on page 122

LIFE Mystery

For your puzzling pleasure: On the next six pages, we present the first-ever
WHODUNIT—a variation on the crime in Alfred Hitchcock's *North by Northwest*

Chapter One: The Action Commences

In this first bit of business, five changes occur, and the larger plot begins to unfold. Pay close attention to the small things—and the big picture.

5
changes

LIFE Mystery

We pause here to allow you to reacquaint yourself with the crime scene.
The tension mounts.

Chapter Two: More Clues

And now five more changes have been made. You have to wonder if Cary Grant is the real culprit—and if the crime spree has even ended.

LIFE Mystery

Another pause as the plot thickens and you prepare yourself for our
final four changes

Everything speeds up now, as Cary seems to sense himself. All eyes are still trained on the floor—all eyes except yours.

MASTER

[Here, puzzles get
a little harder. You'll
need to raise
your game a level.]

Miller Time

This captain is serious about sticking to the rules

A

—

B

—

C

—

D

—

E

1   2   3   4   5

MASTER

9
changes

KEEP
SCORE

❑
❑
❑
❑
❑
❑
❑
❑
❑

⧗
3min 10sec

Answers
on page 123

Smokey and the Bandits

It's a bad habit, but he's trying to kick it

A
—
B
—
C
—
D
—
E

1 | 2 | 3 | 4 | 5

10
changes

⧗

2min 20sec

Answers
on page 123

KEEP SCORE ★ ❏ ❏ ❏ ❏ ❏ ❏ ❏ ❏ ❏ ❏

A Pause in the Action

He's at Bacall's beck and call

THE BIG SLEEP

1   2   3   4   5

9
changes

⧗
2min 10sec

Answers
on page 123

KEEP SCORE ★ ❏ ❏ ❏ ❏ ❏ ❏ ❏ ❏ ❏

Up Against the Wall

Some men act tough, and some men don't have to act—*see*

KISS TOMORROW GOODBYE

A

—

B

—

C

—

D

—

E

1 | 2 | 3 | 4 | 5

10
changes

KEEP
SCORE

❏
❏
❏
❏
❏
❏
❏
❏
❏
❏

⧗

3min 15sec

Answers
on page 123

Swing Low

This cigar aficiando also likes red velvet

A

—

B

—

C

—

D

—

E

1 | 2 | 3 | 4 | 5

11
changes

KEEP
SCORE

❏
❏
❏
❏
❏
❏
❏
❏
❏
❏
❏

⧗
4min 15sec

Answers
on page 123

The President's Go-To Guy

He puts the special back in special forces

THE UNIT/CLIFF LIPSON/CBS/GETTY

9
changes

KEEP
SCORE

❏ ❏ ❏ ❏ ❏ ❏ ❏ ❏ ❏

⧗
2min 45sec

Answers
on page 123

Just One Last Question

You can almost see the suspect start to sweat

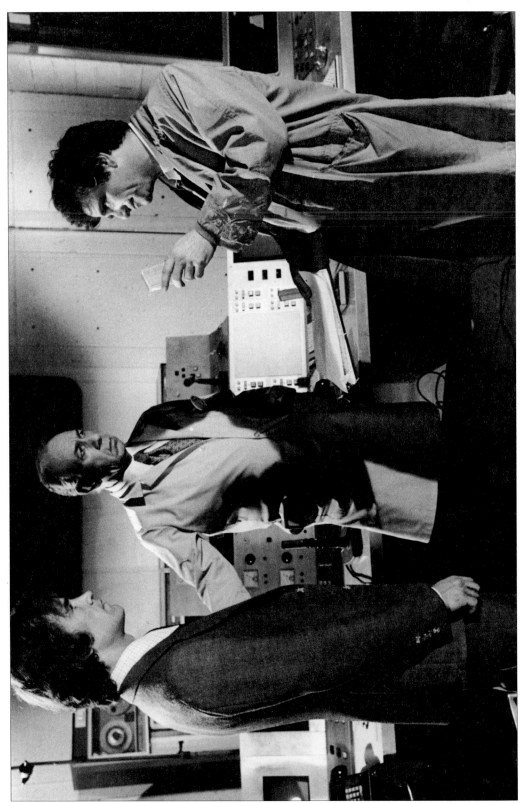

COLUMBO

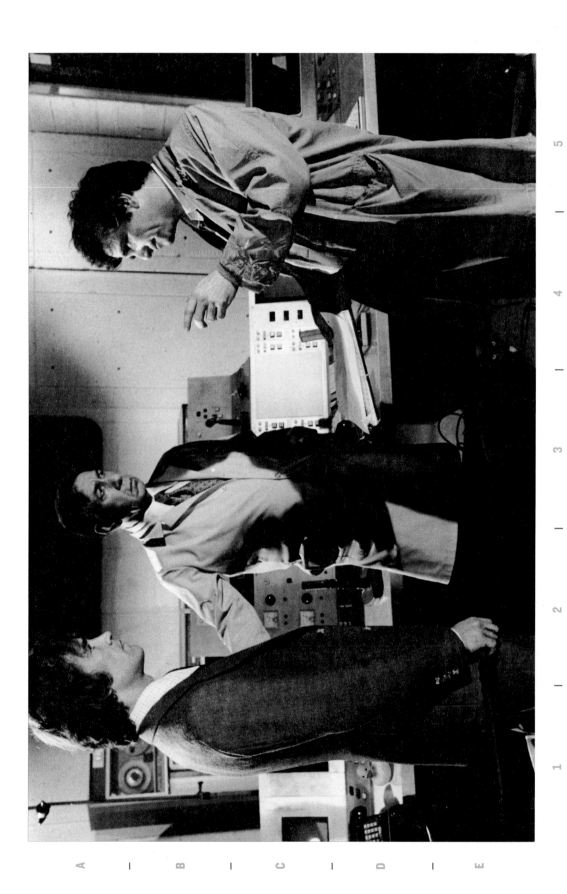

Answers
on page 123

10
changes

KEEP
SCORE

2min 45sec

Heading North by Northwest

Granted, if he doesn't pick up the pace, Cary is going to get dusted

NORTH BY NORTHWEST/MGM

A
—
B
—
C
—
D
—
E

1 | 2 | 3 | 4 | 5

9
changes

⏳

2min 10sec

Answers
on page 124

KEEP SCORE ★ ❑ ❑ ❑ ❑ ❑ ❑ ❑ ❑ ❑ ❑

Watching the Detectives

Ever seen this woman? How 'bout this one?

A
—
B
—
C
—
D
—
E

1 | 2 | 3 | 4 | 5

10
changes

2min 35sec

Answers
on page 124

KEEP SCORE ★ ❏ ❏ ❏ ❏ ❏ ❏ ❏ ❏ ❏ ❏

Calling Dick Tracy! Calling Dick Tracy!

A window of opportunity has opened to get the drop on Flattop

A
—
B
—
C
—
D
—
E

1 | 2 | 3 | 4 | 5

9
changes

⏳
2min 40sec

Answers
on page 124

KEEP SCORE ★ ❏ ❏ ❏ ❏ ❏ ❏ ❏ ❏ ❏

Hands Off the Untouchables

One of these pictures is a little bit two-faced

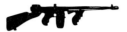

1min 35sec

Answer
on page 124

THE UNTOUCHABLES/CHUCK HODES/PARAMOUNT

Badge of Honor

Only one photo cops to being different

1

2

3

4

5

6

T.J. HOOKER

1min 15sec

Answer
on page 124

The Perils of Mrs. Peel

Clickety-clack, there's a train on the track—and she's all Rigged up

A
—
B
—
C
—
D
—
E

1 | 2 | 3 | 4 | 5

9
changes

⧗
2min 50sec

Answers
on page 124

Avenging Angels

Assemble a picture that's lovely to look at

1min 25sec

Answer
on page 124

KEEP SCORE

Jack's Thirsty

He who owns the water runs the town

CHINATOWN/PARAMOUNT

KEEP SCORE

1min 45sec

Answer
on page 124

Maxwell's Silver Hammer

Get smart and solve this puzzle

A
–
B
–
C
–
D
–
E

1 | 2 | 3 | 4 | 5

9
changes

⧗
3min 35sec

Answers
on page 124

KEEP SCORE ★ ❑ ❑ ❑ ❑ ❑ ❑ ❑ ❑ ❑

Neighborhood Watch

Everyone likes to sneak a peek now and again

REAR WINDOW/SUNSET BOULEVARD/CORBIS

1 | 2 | 3 | 4 | 5

A | B | C | D | E

11
changes

KEEP
SCORE

⏳

3min 55sec

Answers
on page 124

LIFE Mystery

Remember how to play our WHODUNIT? In this first chapter, there are six changes, and a plot starts to build.

Chapter One: Tension in the Air

Someone is clearly not happy about something.
But will it be dealt with mano a mano?

6 changes

1min 25sec

Answers
on page 125

KEEP SCORE ★ ● ● ● ● ● ●

Chapter Two: Escalation

Seven more changes—some of which are of little consequence,
but there is one that means big trouble

7
changes

2min 15sec

Answers
on page 125

KEEP SCORE ★ ● ● ● ● ● ● ●

Chapter Three: Aha!

Here we draw the curtain on a situation that might get violent.
Have you figured out what's in play?

7
changes

3min 55sec

Answers
on page 125

KEEP SCORE ★ ● ● ● ● ● ● ● ●

EXPERT

[

Only serious puzzlers
dare to tread past this point.
Who's in?

]

A Brief for the Defense

With this info, we can Jimmy the case

12
changes

KEEP
SCORE

4min 10sec

Answers
on page 125

What's All This Now?

When an English bobby has a few questions for you,
you'd better be prepared with an answer—or two

THE GIRL WAS YOUNG

A

B

C

D

E

1 2 3 4 5

15
changes

5min **25**sec

Answers
on page 125

KEEP SCORE ★ ❑ ❑ ❑ ❑ ❑ ❑ ❑ ❑ ❑ ❑ ❑ ❑ ❑ ❑ ❑

Do You Feel Lucky?

I know what you're thinkin', punk. You're thinkin' did he hide six really hard changes in this puzzle or only five? Now to tell you the truth, in all this excitement I've forgotten myself.

A

B

C

D

E

1   2   3   4   5

14
changes

⧗

5min 35sec

Answers
on page 125

Use Your Little Gray Cells

Once you've Oriented yourself, find the one that's different

1min 45sec

Answer
on page 125

MURDER ON THE ORIENT EXPRESS/PARAMOUNT PICTURES/MOVIE STILL ARCHIVES

A Matter of Honor

Samurai warriors lived by a code as complicated as this puzzle

侍

RASHOMON/JOHN SPRINGER COLLECTION/CORBIS

1min 15sec

Answer
on page 125

One Well-Connected Puzzle

Pay attention! We're gonna ask questions later.

A
—
B
—
C
—
D
—
E

1   2   3   4   5

15
changes

⧗
4min 50sec

Answers
on page 125

KEEP SCORE ★ ❏ ❏ ❏ ❏ ❏ ❏ ❏ ❏ ❏ ❏ ❏ ❏ ❏ ❏ ❏

So I Says to Him . . .

They're killing a little time in the saloon before the real action begins

MELODIA DE ARRABAL/PARAMOUNT PICTURES

A — B — C — D — E

1 | 2 | 3 | 4 | 5

14
changes

⧗

4min 20sec

Answers
on page 125

Target Practice

The Thin Man's thinner gun has got Asta barking mad

THE THIN MAN/CULVER

A
—
B
—
C
—
D
—
E

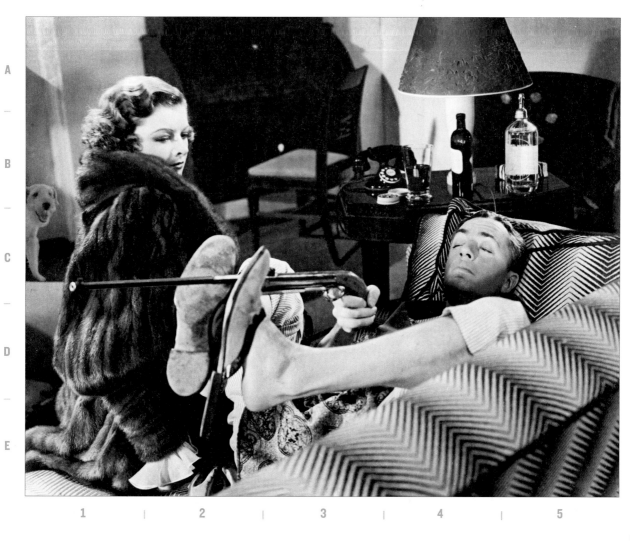

1   2   3   4   5

12 changes

⧗

4min 10sec

Answers
on page 126

KEEP SCORE ★ ☐ ☐ ☐ ☐ ☐ ☐ ☐ ☐ ☐ ☐ ☐ ☐

Cornered

With a run of luck like this, there must be a black cat lurking about

GANGWAY

A
B
C
D
E

1   2   3   4   5

15
changes

⌛
4min 50sec

Answers
on page 126

KEEP SCORE ★ ❏ ❏ ❏ ❏ ❏ ❏ ❏ ❏ ❏ ❏ ❏ ❏ ❏ ❏ ❏

Who's Angry Now?

One man's reasonable doubt is another man's folly . . .
and vice versa

EXPERT

A

B

C

D

E

1   2   3   4   5

13
changes

KEEP
SCORE

☐
☐
☐
☐
☐
☐
☐
☐
☐
☐
☐
☐
☐

⧗

4min **15**sec

Answers
on page 126

PICTURE PUZZLE **LIFE** | **101**

Big Brother Is Watching

And sometimes that's a comforting thought

NCIS/CLIFF LIPSON/CBS/GETTY

14
changes

KEEP
SCORE

⌛
5min 45sec

Answers
on page 126

GENIUS

[Finding a single difference in these puzzles is a challenge. Finding them all might be impossible.]

Give 'Em Enough Rope

They're hanging on every word

ROPE/JOHN SPRINGER COLLECTION/CORBIS

A

B

C

D

E

1   2   3   4   5

14
changes

KEEP
SCORE

❏
❏
❏
❏
❏
❏
❏
❏
❏
❏
❏
❏
❏
❏

⌛
4min 30sec

Answers
on page 126

Beware of Ghosts

If you whisper, they will come

THE GATHERING/MICHAEL DESMOND/CBS/GETTY

15
changes

KEEP
SCORE

❏ ❏ ❏ ❏ ❏ ❏ ❏ ❏ ❏ ❏ ❏ ❏ ❏ ❏ ❏

4min 45sec

Answers
on page 126

A | B | C | D | E

1 2 3 4 5

You Know My Methods, Watson

Nothing clears up a case so much as stating it to another person

A
—
B
—
C
—
D
—
E

1 | 2 | 3 | 4 | 5

17
changes

⏳
5min 35sec

Answers
on page 126

Office Politics

Before they can find the crooks, they need to get along

THE MENTALIST/SONJA FLEMMING/CBS/GETTY

A
—
B
—
C
—
D
—
E

1   2   3   4   5

19
changes

⧗

5min 55sec

Answers
on page 126

KEEP SCORE ★ ☑☑☐☐☐☐☐☐☐☐☐☐☐☐☐☐☐☐☐☐☐☐☐

Mama's Boy

Do you hear a shower running?

14
changes

KEEP
SCORE

❑ ❑ ❑ ❑ ❑ ❑ ❑ ❑ ❑ ❑ ❑ ❑ ❑ ❑

5min 45sec

Answers
on page 127

A | B | C | D | E

1 2 3 4 5

Action on the Set

There are eight million stories in the naked city,
and they're filming one of them

THE NAKED CITY/AP

A

B

C

D

E

1 | 2 | 3 | 4 | 5

12 changes

⏳

5min 25sec

Answers
on page 127

KEEP SCORE ★ ❑ ❑ ❑ ❑ ❑ ❑ ❑ ❑ ❑ ❑ ❑ ❑

Cops on Wheels

These two boys in blue roll in style

15
changes

KEEP
SCORE

❑ ❑
❑ ❑
❑ ❑
❑ ❑
❑ ❑
❑ ❑
❑ ❑
❑

⧗

4min 15sec

Answers
on page 127

Rush Hour

Sometimes it's impossible to find an available cab

BLADE RUNNER/SUNSET BOULEVARD/CORBIS

21
changes

KEEP
SCORE

❑
❑
❑
❑
❑
❑
❑
❑
❑
❑
❑
❑
❑
❑
❑
❑
❑
❑
❑
❑
❑

⧗
6min 45sec

Answers
on page 127

A | B | C | D | E

1   2   3   4   5

[ANSWERS]

Finished already? Let's see how you did.

[INTRODUCTION]

Page 3: **Getting to Know You** No. 1 (A5): Without a pay phone, they're going to wish cell phones had been invented in 1946. No. 2 (B3): Now that her hand is back, she can get a smoke in. No. 3 (D2 to E2): His jacket sleeve has been stretched. Nos. 4, 5, 6, and 7 (D3): Bogart has lost a ring and moved his finger in front of the glass and his fingernail over the paper. Also, the matchsticks are a mite short. Nos. 8 and 9 (D4): In an effort not to let him get ahead, Bacall has dropped a bracelet, and a long, tall lady should have a long, tall drink.

[NOVICE]

Page 7: **Shedding Light on the Case** No. 1 (A4): You'll flip over the department's name. At least the sign's flipped. No. 2 (B2): A picture has decided to flip too. No. 3 (C2): Let's all sing it together: "How old are you now?" No. 4 (D1): Did someone pinch his badge? No. 5 (D2): That rolled-up newspaper has become a bigger tube. No. 6 (D5): His watch has been lifted. No. 7 (E2): Around here, a missing drawer handle counts as a security measure. No. 8 (E5): Part of the lamp neck has disappeared.

Page 8: **Their Job Is Murder** No. 1 (B2): She's got a handle on her flashlight—or perhaps not. No. 2 (C2 to D2): Someone new has shown up behind the police tape. Nos. 3 and 4 (C2 to D3): Not only has he changed the color of his surgical glove, he's also stretched out the fingers. No. 5 (C3): His wife isn't going to be pleased that he lost his wedding ring on the job. No. 6 (D5): The metal luggage has lost a rivet. No. 7 (E3 to E4): They might be able to shine a light on this case after all. No. 8 (E4): Her nails have been painted a lovely shade of lavender, which matches the new glove. But was the nail polish applied pre- or postmortem?

Page 10: **Masonic Rituals** No. 1 (A1 to A3): The wood paneling has gained an inch or two in height. No. 2 (A5 to C5): The curtains have been drawn. No. 3 (B1): Not only has her head disappeared, her hat is now floating in the air. No. 4 (B2): He had his hair restyled during a recess. No. 5 (C3): Given the spectators in this courtroom, she may have thrown her pearls before swine. No. 6 (D4 to E4): A bigger coffee cup means all that much more caffeine. No. 7 (E2): Who's reading the paperback courtroom drama? No. 8 (E3): And did Perry misplace his reading glasses? No. 9 (E5): *Hmm*, these books leave no reflections.

Page 12: **Falling Dominoes** No. 1 (A2 to B3): The sheriff's portrait needs to be righted. No. 2 (A3): The brim of his cap looms larger. No. 3 (A4 to B4): The trophy is spinning around. No. 4 (A5): The frosted glass needs new signage. No. 5 (C2): Another lamp stem bites the dust. No. 6 (C4): The lock for the file cabinet

drawer has switched sides. No. 7 (C5): Batman he ain't, but his utility belt has added a pouch. No. 8 (E1): Both the chair and the suspect are about to take a tumble. No. 9 (E5): This refrigerator can hold more soda. But not beer—never beer.

Page 14: **This Is the City** Nos. 1 and 2 (A1): The reward has gone up, but so too the number of misspellings. No. 3 (D2): The mugs have switched their shots. No. 4 (D4 to E3): He must have dropped his pencil. No. 5 (D4 to E4): That's an interesting bracelet he's wearing. No. 6 (D5): A buttonhole has been lost. No. 7 (E1 to E2): This time the reflectionless object is a cigarette pack. Our puzzle master must be stuck in a rut. We'll talk to him once we pin him down.

Page 16: **Whose Charade Is It?** No. 1 (A2): The letter *L* is now an *E*, and we're greatly relieved. No. 2 (A3 to B4): The tile must have fallen out and been replaced—backward. No. 3 (C1 to D1): With one hand, he offers her a flower. No. 4 (E1 to E2): With the other, he records everything she says. No. 5 (E2 to E5): The tabletop is now noticeably thicker. No. 6 (E4): Now that's quite a rare stamp.

Page 18: **Five Birds of a Feather . . .** Photo No. 3 has a rebel bird.

Page 19: **Ectoplasmic Mischief** In photo No. 5, there's a picture with a difference.

Page 20: **Lunge, Parry, Thrust** No. 1 (A4): In an emergency, ring that bell. No. 2 (A5): A crow has landed before the storm. No. 3 (B1): A shorter sword makes for a shorter lunge. No. 4 (D1): The chest has slid across the deck. Is the ship keeling over? No. 5 (D2 to D3): Now her cape has more drape. No. 6 (D5): Does anyone need a hand? No. 7 (E3): Miss Marple's fancy footwork moves in slo-mo these days.

Page 22: **You're Pretty as a Picture, Laura** No. 1 (A2 to B3): The sconce and its shadow have suffered a little compression. Nos. 2 and 3 (A3 to C4): Laura's portrait has been stretched and flipped. No. 4 (B5): This light fixture has lost a glass bauble. No. 5 (C1 to D1): The longer umbrella handle offers a better grip. No. 6 (D1): As

if by magic, the left end of the table has been erased. No. 7 (D3): One of these andirons has met its end. No. 8 (E2): The bowl has recessed.

Page 24: Lady Be Good No. 1 (A3 to B3): The lampshade is spreading out. No. 2 (B2 to C2): One of the metal curves has swerved out of the way. No. 3 (B4): The lady's earring hangs lower. No. 4 (C1): The back of the couch has returned. No. 5 (C3): The vase now holds one more rose. No. 6 (C3 to D3): It looks like this candleholder was left out in the purple rain. No. 7 (D4): Some of the wooden scrollwork has fallen off.

Page 25: Service for Two No. 1 (A2): A ghostly figure has appeared in the painting on the wall. No. 2 (A3 to B4): The tapestry is a little bit shifty. No. 3 (A5): This candle burns upward, not downward. No. 4 (A5 to B5): What is that menacing shadow lurking in the background? No. 5 (B3 to B4): A candelabra has been sold to pay for this hospitality. No. 6 (C4): In springtime, tea service spouts begin sprouting across the nation.

Page 26: Disappearing Act No. 1 (A2 to A3): An ambitious wood panel is stretching upward. No. 2 (B1 to C2): The lady really is vanishing. No. 3 (B5): An extra insignia has been placed on this panel. No. 4 (C4): Now why did she take off her ring? No. 5 (C5): The latch for the sliding door is MIA. No. 6 (D3): He thinks she has the makings of a great catcher so he's teaching her a few baseball signals before the spring tryouts. No. 7 (D4): His bow tie is shedding some spots. No. 8 (E4): Is there a seamstress in the audience who can sew on a button?

Page 28: Fiddling About No. 1 (C2): If she could read upside down, the Nanny might just find a clue. Nah, she's too busy laughing. No. 2 (C2 to C3): She's added a button to her ensemble. No. 3 (C5): The pedestal is now monolithic. No. 4 (D2): It's a tippy, tippy stool. No. 5 (D4): The suspected murder weapon has been mysteriously removed from the crime scene. No. 6 (E1): Could this kid be the son of Big Foot? No. 7 (E1 to E5): The ratty rug keeps getting bigger and bigger. No. 8 (E5): It's a bit late to take up the violin.

Page 30: High Society No. 1 (A3): If you're a celebrity-spotter spotter, you might just notice Dominic Dunne hiding behind the column. No. 2 (A5): Never one to hide from his public, Truman Capote is just relaxing over a good meal. No. 3 (B2): This smile is not a nice smile. No. 4 (B3): A grommet has popped out of the wall. No. 5 (C4): She's protecting herself with more pearls. No. 6 (D4 to E4): And she's added some liquid fortification. No. 7 (E3): On the other hand, this glass must be afraid of the veiled lady, because it's shrinking.

Page 32: Truth Seeker No. 1 (A1 to B1): Behind the scenes, maintenance has been busy fixing a bent shaft. No. 2 (B2 to C2): And part of the wheel has been filled in. No. 3 (B3): The fugitive has a good head of Elvis hair now. No. 4 (C3 to D3): And he definitely has two good hands. Nos. 5 and 6 (D2 to E3): The latticework and a crack have been repaired just in time. No. 7 (D3): But unfortunately, the step has a new crack. No. 8 (D5 to E5): In his haste, the one-armed man appears to have dropped his prosthetic device. No. 9 (E5): Obviously, the construction firm didn't use shrink-resistant materials when building this place.

Page 34: Band Practice No. 1 (A1): An extra sconce provides more illumination for the band. No. 2 (A3 to A5): The doorway's been raised for the taller members. No. 3 (B2 to C2): We've heard of illuminated maps, but this is a little ridiculous. No. 4 (B4): Funny, wasn't his wound on the other side of his head? No. 5 (C2): Bet you didn't know Bogart played the flute. No. 6 (C5 to D5): We know who plays sax around here. No. 7 (D3 to E4): Is Mary Astor taking up the electric guitar? No. 8 (D4): Peter Lorre seems a natural as a stickman. No. 9 (D5): At least this time a ring is appearing instead of vanishing. No. 10 (E1): The black bird—it's the stuff that dreams are made of.

Page 36: A Dogged Investigation

4	3
2	1

Page 37: Dreaming of Manderlay

3	1
4	2

Page 38: Captain of the Queen's Navy No. 1 (A1): Apparently being Alec Guinness is a contagious condition and the gent in the corner has caught the bug. No. 2 (A3): Doesn't she look stylish in her fedora? No. 3 (B1): After a little carpentry work, the door fits snugly against its sill. No. 4 (B2): Forget the flat feet—he's wearing a reporter's badge. No. 5 (C4): Now hear this! Return the glass to the captain immediately. No. 6 (D2): First you lift your right foot up in the air, then you stare around grumpily and complain that it ain't fair.

Page 40: Peekaboo, I See You No. 1 (A2 to B2): Foil or suspect, his shrinking status means he no longer measures up against the grade. No. 2 (A3): On the other hand, our third man has had a late growth spurt. Nos. 3 and 4 (A5): The numbers have traded places while someone loses his

hair. No. 5 (B1): This is not a good look for him. No. 6 (B3): His shirt has taken on a royal hue. No. 7 (C1): A prankster is still messing with the measurements. No. 8 (C5): It takes guts to steal a watch during a lineup. No. 9 (E4): Even a scrap of paper can confuse a potential witness.

[WHODUNIT]

Pages 42 to 47: North by Northeast
No. 1 (A1 to A2): The old gray bridge ain't what it used to be. No. 2 (B3): A rubbernecking waiter has stopped to watch the misdeed. Nos. 3 and 4 (C3): Not only has our original suspect dropped the knife, someone has also dropped a second glass on the coffee table. No. 5 (E4 to E5): This lady has no visible means of support. Nos. 6 and 7 (B5): One man's taken a powder and another appears to have a dagger in his hand. No. 8 (C1): She's lost her bracelet. Nos. 9 and 10 (D2): Our victim has suddenly donned a wig, while one woman has grown so comfortable around crime scenes that she's slipped off her shoe. No. 11 (B3 to B4): It used to be called flash-bulb journalism. Nos. 12 and 13 (B4): He grunted in pain when the knife found its new target. No. 14 (B5): Another man has left the building. No. 15 (C2): Cary is ready to duke it out with one and all. And our nominee for the new suspect is the gray-haired man who departed in haste!

[MASTER]

Page 49: Miller Time No. 1 (A2): Hopefully no one in lockup will notice the opening in the bars. No. 2 (B2): The precinct is so old, the writing is fading from the walls. No. 3 (B4): Sometimes a conversation is so serious you have to put your glasses on. No. 4 (C3 to D2): His hands are coming in for a landing. No. 5 (D1 to E1): Don't look now, Barney, but someone's got your gun. Nos. 6 and 7 (E2): The thirsty trophy has spun around to face the frosty bottle of beer. No. 8 (E3 to E4): Stealing watches seems to be a common problem among detectives. No. 9 (E5): That tie is way too long.

Page 50: Smokey and the Bandits
No. 1 (A1): A portion of the beam's filigree is taking a spin. No. 2 (A4 to B4): You've heard of high hopes? This is a high hat. No. 3 (B2 to C2): His nickname is "Shifty." No. 4 (B4): Mr. High Hat has lost his cigar. No. 5 (B5 to C5): They'll let anyone in this joint. No. 6 (C2): With all the smoke, a cigar is kind of redundant. No. 7 (D5): He's put the cork back in. No. 8 (D5 to E5): Drink as much as you want—there's always more bourbon in this bottle. Nos. 9 and 10 (E2): He's popped a button, and the bartender's plopped down another glass.

Page 52: A Pause in the Action No. 1 (A1): A carpenter has extended the cabinet on the left. No. 2 (A2): She's waited too long, because someone's coming down the stairs. No. 3 (A5): Wrong movie, Mr. Lorre! Nos. 4 and 5 (C4): The Surgeon General has warned that smoking is hazardous to your health, Mr. Bogart. But the sideburn seems perfectly

safe. No. 6 (C5): That's one big cushion. No. 7 (E2): Her bracelet has been nicked. No. 8 (E3): So cut the ropes already. No. 9 (E5): Finally! He's starting to shed the cords.

Page 54: Up Against the Wall No. 1 (A2 to A3): He has inflatable hair. Who knew? No. 2 (A3): Be careful: When her eyebrow moves like that, she's about to make some kind of arch comment. No. 3 (A5): It took us hours to chisel our logo into this brick. We hope you appreciate the effort. Nos. 4, 5, and 6 (B1): While the barrel of the gun may be longer, its end is all plugged up now. Also, the shadow is no longer moving across his trigger finger. No. 7 (B4 to C4): Her thumb has a deeper grasp of the situation. No. 8 (C2): Like a lot of the other actors in this book, Mr. Cagney appears to be prone to losing his buttons. No. 9 (C4): Her skirt hugs her waist so tightly, she doesn't need that belt. No. 10 (D5): Two bricks in the wall have forged a close alliance.

Page 56: Swing Low No. 1 (A4 to B4): Sometimes it's better to just close the curtains and get some privacy. No. 2 (B2): The face of Joan Collins is starting to morph into that of the original party girl, Evelyn Nesbit. Nos. 3 and 4 (B3): She's dropped the match, and his cigar is wilting. Nos. 5 and 6 (B5): Watch out! Her foot packs quite a wallop. That's probably why the wood paneling had to be repaired. No. 7 (D1): The curtain is dangling a little lower. No. 8 (D2): And with all the spinning around, the quill is starting to feel ill. No. 9 (D3 to D4): His vest is inching down. No. 10 (D5): The chair is losing its standing. No. 11 (E3): He's got one of those trendy sliding ashtrays.

Page 58: The President's Go-To Guy
No. 1 (A2): The cross is reaching up to Heaven. No. 2 (B1): A candle has gone AWOL. No. 3 (B3 to C3): He doesn't have a hand to spare. No. 4 (B4): The center candle stands above the rest. No. 5 (B5): Now all the candles are lit. No. 6 (C4): The candelabra is floating in the air. No. 7 (D3): The boot is a size too large. No. 8 (D3 to E3): One of the sergeant major's legs is a step behind. No. 9 (D5): The back of this pew is a bit different from the others.

Page 60: Just One Last Question
No. 1 (A3): He's going to the same hair specialist as Columbo—not that that's necessarily a good idea. No. 2 (B3): He lost his badge somewhere along the way. Do you think that's going to slow up the investigation? No. 3 (B4): Did Columbo drop a cassette (and possible evidence) out of his hand? Nah, couldn't be. No. 4 (C2): The bright spot on that top console knob has shifted from the left to the right. Nos. 5 and 6 (D1): The telephone has gained an extra row of buttons, and a bath toy has floated into the picture. No. 7 (D2): The microphone cord has been cut. No. 8 (D5): In order to discourage smoking, all the ashtrays have been removed. No. 9 (E1 to E2): Is that a police baton he's hiding? No. 10 (E3 to E4): It's nice that they can keep a pet at the lab.

Page 62: Heading North by Northwest
No. 1 (A1): The upper-left wing is longer now. No. 2 (A1 to B1): Tut, tut—a wing strut has snapped off. No. 3 (A1 to B3): It looks like the plane is retreating. No. 4 (B1 to C2): And its wheels are a mite too big. No. 5 (B3): The upper-right wing tip has been stretched out. Nos. 6 and 7 (C4): Mr. Grant's tie has lost its label, and his jacket sleeve has grown. No. 8 (C5): The ground is sloping upward. No. 9 (E4): Cary and his shadow are parting company.

Page 64: Watching the Detectives
No. 1 (A1 to B2): The lamp has been removed for use in another scene. No. 2 (A2): I wouldn't chance telling him, but it looks like a certain detective is losing his hair. No. 3 (A2 to B2): But his mustache gives him a certain devil-may-care air. No. 4 (A3 to B3): The folding screen won't fold here anymore. No. 5 (A4 to B5): Another wrestler is getting ready for the ring. No. 6 (B4 to C4): This detective appears to be studying electromagnetism on the side. How else could he so casually polarize his tie? No. 7 (C3): Blame another one on the detective's side interest in physics: Just who is he looking for—the blonde or her sister from a mirror-image universe? No. 8 (C5): His badge is pointing south. No. 9 (D4): Even with his mathematical skills, he still loses his buttons. No. 10 (E5): This must be a mood lamp—wonder what purple means.

Page 66: Calling Dick Tracy! Calling Dick Tracy!
No. 1 (A1): The bricks appear to be splitting up. No. 2 (A2): On the other hand, two of the stones above the window's head jamb have decided to form a more perfect union. No. 3 (A3 to A4): Tracy's hat sure is swell. Or at least it's swelling up. Nos. 4 and 5 (A5 to D5): The wall and Tracy's arm are being radically stretched, and a window has vanished. Nos. 6 and 7 (D2): Judging by the missing hat, some crook has fled the apartment. At the same time, Flattop has moved his arm closer to his body. No. 8 (D3): Tracy has a new tiny, squeaky companion. No. 9 (E4): He'd better keep a close eye on this crack in the ledge; it appears to be getting bigger by the minute.

Page 68: Hands Off the Untouchables
We're not going to say anything, but there may be some illegal cloning going on in photo No. 4.

Page 69: Badge of Honor
T. J. Hooker's badge in photo No. 1 points the wrong way.

Page 70: The Perils of Mrs. Peel
No. 1 (A4 to B4): The little engine that could is sure belching a lot of smoke. No. 2 (B4): The headlight guides the way. No. 3 (C3): That's what we like to see in a locomotive—a positive attitude. Nos. 4 and 5 (C4): There's no way to get a handle on this train now that it's gone through a number inversion. No. 6 (D2): In all the confusion, Mr. Steed has gained an extra watch. Now he has all the time in the world. No. 7 (D2 to E2): One rope down, a lot more to go. *Choo-choo!* Nos. 8 and 9 (E1): A mysterious stranger casts a shadow on the whole proceedings. Did he cut the track?

Page 72: Avenging Angels

6	3
5	1
2	4

Page 73: Jack's Thirsty

6	5
4	2
1	3

Page 74: Maxwell's Silver Hammer
No. 1 (A2): He's slipped out of one of the ties that bind. No. 2 (A4): Max's other hand may still be manacled, but it looks like he's been listening to the Weaver's old song "If I Had a Hammer." Nos. 3 and 4 (B1): A ship with four smokestacks? That sounds familiar. In the meantime, the porthole is down a bolt. No. 5 (B3): Agent 99, do you know where Max got his brand-new diamond stud earring? No. 6 (C3): It takes only one bad link in the chain. No. 7 (D1): The rope has shed part of its shadow. No. 8 (D1 to E2): We know one mad scientist who's ready to trumpet his accomplishments. No. 9 (D4 to D5): Agent 99 has the means to start enforcing a little discipline around here.

Page 76: Neighborhood Watch
No. 1 (A3): He's just a friendly Greenwich Village rodent. No. 2 (A4): Did you spot one of the tools of our photographer's trade next to the kitchen sink? Nos. 3 and 4 (A5 to B5): The angle of the open window gives us an unexpected reflection of a party in the building across the courtyard. No. 5 (B1): The cabinet doors are blending together. No. 6 (B2): It's a good thing he's not going to need his wheelchair too much longer—it's starting to fall apart. Wait a minute! Do you know something we don't? No. 7 (C1 to D1): What's in the trunk? Don't ask. Nos. 8 and 9 (D4): She's lost a bead from her bracelet but gained a wedding ring. No. 10 (E1): Even her pointed toe exudes grace. No. 11 (E4): A movie about a LIFE photographer should have a copy of the magazine laying around somewhere.

[WHODUNIT]

Pages 78 to 83: The Love (and Death) Motel
No. 1 (A4): Think pink! No. 2 (B1 to E1): People who open doors without knocking shouldn't be surprised by what they find. No. 3 (B2 to C2): He's wearing one of the new inflatable collars. No. 4 (B4): Looks like he's getting a teensy-weensy bit upset. No. 5 (C1): Let there be more light switches. No. 6 (E2): Is that a pistol in his pocket, or is he just scared of company? No. 7 (A4): An electrician has been busy converting this sconce into a hanging light. No. 8 (C4 to D4): A sunbeam has disappeared. Nos. 9 and 10 (D1): Her shift has shifted downward, and the door lock has been hocked. No. 11 (D1 to E1): Her legs just got leggier. No. 12 (D5 to E4): Didn't his mother warn him not to play with pointy objects? No. 13 (E2): Putting away his gun may have been a mistake. No. 14 (A1 to A2): The door has gained some height. Nos. 15 (C1): Her pearls are down a strand. No. 16 (C2): Security has been further compromised with the loss of another lock. No. 17 (C3): It may be too late for placating gestures. Nos. 18 and 19 (D1): She's packing, too, and her dress has been returned to its original hem length. No. 20 (E1): She's looking more relaxed. And our pick—pun intended—as the most likely to commit mayhem is the dark-haired fellow who likes to chop his own ice. But we're also keeping our eyes on the pistol-packing mama.

[EXPERT]

Page 85: A Brief for the Defense No. 1 (A1 to A2): This courtroom finally has an exit. No. 2 (B3): Jimmy's hair is receding. No. 3 (B4 to C4): Someone in the gallery is feeling somewhat fidgety. Nos. 4 and 5 (B5 to C5): The guy with the wide collars has a twin—or an alien clone—and Mr. Creepy wants a better view of the action. No. 6 (D2): The rail has been fused together. Nos. 7 and 8 (D4): Not only has his tie gone down a stripe, now his briefcase won't lock anymore. No. 9 (E1): This post is not as shiny as it once was. No. 10 (E2): And another has been relocated. No. 11 (E3): His briefcase is getting strapped down. No. 12 (E4): And a metal loop has broken off.

Page 86: What's All This Now? No. 1 (A2): The entranceway lamp has lost a decorative element. No. 2 (A2 to A3): Also, the lamp's support seems to have vanished. No. 3 (B1 to C1): The sun has bleached his hair blond. No. 4 (B3): My, what big ears you have! No. 5 (B4): His uniform has an extra number on it now. Nos. 6, 7, and 8 (C2): While one man has misplaced his glasses, another has dropped his camera and is starting to look more and more like Hitchcock. No. 9 (C2 to D3): He's getting a lot of time to practice with the yo-yo. No. 10 (C3 to C4): Flowers just seem to make the day a little brighter. No. 11 (C4): This sign has a rebellious *C*. No. 12 (C5): What's a little less mortar between stones? No. 13 (D2): At least this man has gained a button. No. 14 (D3): Doesn't this belt belong in the evidence room? No. 15 (E5): The feathered stoolie has been set free.

Page 88: Do You Feel Lucky? No. 1 (A2): The stack has bottomed out. No. 2 (B1 to C1): It looks like the shack is getting a little repair work done. No. 3 (B3): Finger-pointing is probably not going to work as well as a gun. No. 4 (B5 to C5): The hill is subsiding. No. 5 (C2): When the conduit broke, the shack lost power. No. 6 (C2 to D2): The crossbeam is situated behind the post now. Nos. 7 and 8 (C3): Continuity alert! Clint is down a pocket and a hand. No. 9 (C4 to C5): The roof has been extended. No. 10 (D1): The rabbit's getting out while the getting is good. No. 11 (D5): We call this rock "Big Sylvia." No. 12 (E1): This one here is "Baby Sylvia." No. 13 (E2 to E3): Clint's shadow is slanting downward as the day grows long. No. 14 (E4): The rock that's scampering around is named "Fred." We're not sure why.

Page 90: Use Your Little Gray Cells The casting in photo No. 1 seems a little confused.

Page 91: A Matter of Honor The costume in photo No. 5 is shedding its design.

Page 92: One Well-Connected Puzzle
No. 1 (A2): Without any streetlights, New York would be a very dark place indeed. No. 2 (A3 to A4): There's more pork in his porkpie hat. No. 3 (A4): Part of the building behind the bridge has been demolished. No. 4 (A5 to C5): The taller they come, the harder they fall. Nos. 5 and 6 (B1): Come on, enter. You know you want to. But don't let the badge fall off your hat. Nos. 7 and 8 (B2): This car is down a light, and his mock turtleneck has turned purple. No. 9 (B3 to B4): One of the stripes on his tie has taken a hike. No. 10 (B4): An officer has gone undercover. No. 11 (C1): Rifles down! No. 12 (C1 to C2): His hands are both in sync. No. 13 (C1 to D2): And now that his feet are ready, it's dance fever time. No. 14 (C5): This gives new meaning to the term *pop a wheelie.* No. 15 (D4): Just because the barrel has been snubbed, doesn't mean the gun's a toy.

Page 94: So I Says to Him . . . No. 1 (A1): Three gourds are down to two. No. 2 (A3): The poster's been removed. No. 3 (A4): His hat is fatter. No. 4 (A5): The window must have a magical reversa-pane. No. 5 (B1 to B2): One of the bartenders has gone off duty. No. 6 (B3): But don't worry—another one has shown up. No. 7 (B3 to B4): He liked his friend's mustache so much, he copied it. No. 8 (B4 to C4): His tailor removed the buttonhole from his jacket. No. 9 (C2): Is that a Wembley gun he's hiding in his jacket? No. 10 (C3): He gave his hankie to a friend in need. No. 11 (C4): Someone's inked in part of his tie. No. 12 (C5): The tongue of this handkerchief is hanging down. No. 13 (D2): Yeah, that's right, another missing button. No. 14 (D3 to E3): Whose shot glass is this?

Page 96: **Target Practice** No. 1 (A1): No doorknob, no way out. No. 2 (A4 to A5): Does a wider lampshade provide more shade? No. 3 (A4 to B4): Let's pop the cork. Never mind, we already did. No. 4 (B1 to C1): *Bark, bark!* Asta doesn't like guns. No. 5 (B3): The drawer pull was pulled out. Nos. 6 and 7 (B4): This phone can no longer dial zeros, but at least the glass can hold more drink. No. 8 (C1 to C2): That's one long barrel. Nos. 9 and 10 (C3): The chair leg has lost its shadow, and the cord's been cut. No. 11 (C4): Now, that's a close shave. No. 12 (E2): He's quite a heel.

Page 98: **Cornered** No. 1 (A1): The wall has lost a bullet hole. No. 2 (A1 to A2): Things are looking up at least for the wall; it's been given some new trim. No. 3 (A3): Stealing doorknobs seems to be the in crime these days. No. 4 (B1): Just when things seem at their worst, you find out that you have a bigger table. No. 5 (B2): That's quite a hat. No. 6 (B3): His tommy gun has lost its sight. No. 7 (B5 to C5): Black cats don't have to be an ominous omen, do they? No. 8 (C2): Oh, great! His gun is shrinking. Did he pick up the one carved from soap? No. 9 (C3 to D3): Which way should she look? Which way should she look? No. 10 (C5): When he finds that bullet hole in his hat, he's going to realize what a lucky guy he is. No. 11 (D1): A table leg was blasted away during an earlier round of shooting. No. 12 (D2): Okay, this isn't funny—who borrowed my gun? No. 13 (D3 to E3): The table has taken such a pounding, it's now got a whole lotta lumps. No. 14 (D5 to E5): The wood block is twice its former size. No. 15 (E2): Did they have cell phones back then?

Page 100: **Who's Angry Now?** No. 1 (A5): The molding is climbing up the wall. Nos. 2 and 3 (B2): After the carpenters deepened the top of the bench, they also removed one of the vertical supports. No. 4 (B4): He has a pencil in his pocket just in case. No. 5 (B5): The armrest is missing. No. 6 (C2): The fold of his shirtsleeve has grown. No. 7 (C3): When did he take his watch off? No. 8 (C3 to D4): He did have a wallet under there earlier, didn't he? No. 9 (C4): The photo has become the antithesis of its former self. No. 10 (C5): What is the chain of custody on this switchblade? No. 11 (D5): Someone smokes way too much. Nos. 12 and 13 (E3 to E5): The table was extended just in time to hold the pair of glasses.

Page 102: **Big Brother Is Watching** Nos. 1 and 2 (A2): Three of these clocks are duplicating their original roles . . . but one is not. No. 3 (A2 to A3): This rail wasn't here when we came down the stairs. No. 4 (A3): A bigger flat screen reveals better clues. No. 5 (A4): The letter *L* is sticking on someone's keyboard. No. 6 (B2 to C3): Two more people came on shift. Nos. 7 and 8 (B5): The pink search area appears to be smaller now, and the arrow is pointing in the opposite direction. No. 9 (C3): The table leg can't be extended any higher. No. 10 (D2): A wheel has rolled away. No. 11 (D3 to D4): His jacket has been let out. No. 12 (D5): The control palette is climbing up the screen. No. 13 (E2): His sleeve is longer. No. 14 (E5): The baseboard is widening.

Page 105: **Give 'Em Enough Rope** Nos. 1 and 2 (A1): As the lights go on in one building, another climbs higher into the sky. No. 3 (A2): A DC-3 has taken off from Idlewild. No. 4 (A3 to B3): He can't decide where to look. No. 5 (A4 to B4): A plastic surgeon has been busy with this fellow. No. 6 (B1): Jimmy Stewart does not look good in drag. Let me repeat that: Jimmy Stewart does not look good in drag. No. 7 (B2): Something has shocked her. No. 8 (B4): His handkerchief has one less point. No. 9 (B5): On the other hand, Jimmy's has three points now. No. 10 (C5): Jimmy's sleeve has been pulled down. No. 11 (D4): Where did he get that bit of rope? No. 12 (D5): The furniture is being moved out of the way for the lost dance scene. (Hitchcock had it edited from the film.) No. 13 (E1): Her dress is longer. No. 14 (E2 to E3): For some reason, he's standing taller.

Page 106: **Beware of Ghosts** No. 1 (A1 to C1): Can't they see that apparition floating in the hallway? Why aren't they screaming? No. 2 (A2): The numbers on the clockface have vanished. No. 3 (A3 to A4): The chandelier has more crystals now. Nos. 4 and 5 (A4 to B4): We're not sure if the policeman outside the window is from this world, but we're certain the altered wood trim is. No. 6 (B1 to C1): There's a hole in the tray, dear Liza, dear Liza. No. 7 (B2): The cutout in the door of the clock has been sealed up. No. 8 (B5 to C5): The handle must have fallen off the fireplace screen. No. 9 (C2): Electricians have removed an outlet. No. 10 (C3): She's lost her necklace. No. 11 (C4): One handle is floating in the air. No. 12 (D2): Termites may have eaten away at the table leg. No. 13 (D4): She's beeperless now. No. 14 (D5 to E5): A child has disappeared. No. 15 (E4 to E5): The dictionary looks as if it's ready to float off.

Page 108: **You Know My Methods, Watson** No. 1 (A1 to D1): The curtain has been pulled forward. Nos. 2 and 3 (A5): The hinge has been removed from the box, and the blowgun now hangs from the molding. Nos. 4 and 5 (B2): Watson has lost a dot from his tie and a button from his vest. No. 6 (B4): The revolver has extended its barrel. No. 7 (B4 to B5): The numbers on the radio dial have switched places. No. 8 (B5): And the radio has lost a knob. No. 9 (B5 to C5): The tabletop is stretching to the right. No. 10 (C2): Sherlock's pencil gets longer when no one's looking at it. No. 11 (C4): The title on the spine of the book in the nook is slipping down. No. 12 (D1 to E1): The bottom of the table leg is missing. Nos. 13 and 14 (D2): A vent is gone, and the cord to the jack has been cut. No. 15 (D2 to D3): Who took the oscilloscope screen? No. 16 (D3): The braid on his sleeve has been worn away. No. 17 (E5): The chairback is broken.

Page 110: **Office Politics** No. 1 (A1): The cubicle frame has been revised. No. 2 (A3): The second floor has lost one of its supports. Structural engineers have been called in for an emergency evaluation. Nos. 3 and 4 (A4): One of the track lights has been turned on, and another has been installed. Nos. 5 and 6 (A4 to B4): The exit sign has exited, and the fire

alarm light is moving up in the world. No. 7 (A5): A lag bolt is missing. Better let the engineers know when they get here. Nos. 8 and 9 (B2): She's changed her camisole and lost her necklace. No. 10 (B3 to C3): His eyes have swapped positions. No. 11 (B4): A safe without a handle isn't very safe. No. 12 (B5): The lamp has swiveled upward. Nos. 13 and 14 (C4): A column of buttons has drifted away, and someone is either a fan of old movies or likes to play our puzzles online. Nos. 15 and 16 (D3): Another chair leg bites the dust, while two drawers form a perfect union. No. 17 (D5 to E5): Meanwhile, these two drawers are feuding over territory. No. 18 (E2): It's a good thing his shoe is soleless, not him. No. 19 (E4): This chair needs some leverage.

Page 112: **Mama's Boy** No. 1 (A1): A bird has glided away. No. 2 (A2): He should be careful about standing on the roof like that. Nos. 3 and 4 (B3): The eave has lost a bracket and the window its mullions. No. 5 (C1): Does the new window fit the design? No. 6 (C2 to D2): That woman is a restless soul. No. 7 (C3 to D3): At least that man has a shorter distance from which to fall. No. 8 (C5): A crow has landed on the tree. No. 9 (D4): Wait a minute! This guy looks exactly the same as the other two. Except he's turning his head the other way. No. 10 (D4 to E4): And he's a giant. Nos. 11 and 12 (E2): Hitchcock is making an appearance, and someone's rubbed vanishing cream into this column. No. 13 (E4): This planter can levitate. No. 14 (E5): One stone has turned into two.

Page 114: **Action on the Set** No. 1 (B2): The bridge is cracking. That can't be a good thing, can it? No. 2 (B5): Reports indicate that a water tower was stolen from a building across the river this morning. No. 3 (C1): Quick, change lanes! You don't want to be riding behind this wheelless truck. No. 4 (C1 to C2): Not only does the bridge have a crack, it's dropped a strut. Nos. 5 and 6 (C3): Without all its cooling vents, big lights like this one overheat very quickly. And without its bracket, it'll fall over even quicker. No. 7 (C4 to D4): A car has been parked farther down the street. Nos. 8 and 9 (C5): This building has lost a balcony and a window—not that anyone lives there these days. No. 10 (D4 to D5): He's put on a cap to help keep himself warm. Nos. 11 and 12 (D5): Two windows have been combined, and a white Chevy has been driven away.

Page 116: **Cops on Wheels** No. 1 (A1 to B1): Was this tombstone here a moment ago? I don't think so. No. 2 (A2 to B2): Let's say it all together now: There's no such thing as ghosts. There's no such thing as ghosts. No. 3 (A3): Either vandals have stolen this little marker, or it has entered into the gravestone protection program. No. 4 (A5): This monument says it all, doesn't it? No. 5 (B1 to B2): If he just took the time to look at what's going on behind him in his wider-angle rear-view mirror, he'd be long gone. No. 6 (B2): How cute—he's wearing his battery-powered brim-lowering helmet. No. 7 (C1): Just in case he gets lost, he has the extended version of the City of Los Angeles map. No. 8 (C1 to C2): His pant leg has been stripped of its stripes. No. 9 (C2): The star is taking a spin around the gas tank. No. 10 (C3): No brand labels here, mate. No. 11 (C4): With a leggier boot, this cop is catwalk-worthy. Nos. 12 and 13 (D3): The brake line has snaked behind a chrome bar, and a fender-bender must have truncated that fender. No. 14 (D5): Another chrome bar has jumped in front of the

fender on the right. No. 15 (E4 to E5): Sad to say, but it looks like this bike is coming down with vanishing-shadow syndrome. There is no known cure; however, the affliction does have its own telethon.

Page 118: **Rush Hour** No. 1 (A1): The blue signage has been shortened. No. 2 (A4 to B4): It's never too late for an *S* to become an 8. No. 3 (A4 to B5): The light display has turned blue. No. 4 (A5): A bulb has burned out. No. 5 (B1): If you knew kanji like we know kanji, you'd realize that this sign says "Blade Runner." We hope. No. 6 (B2): The flaps on Harrison's jacket collar have united. No. 7 (B3): We've added a diagonal to the *P* to turn it into an *R*. No. 8 (B4): And the arch has gone on a march. No. 9 (C1): The neon sign is feeling a little purplish. Nos. 10 and 11 (C2): Where did he get his light saber, and when did the black squares invade the white one between them? No. 12 (C3): That *T* has got a brand-new slant. No. 13 (C4): The cab is feeling a little ILL. No. 14 (C4 to C5): The roof sign is lurching to the right. No. 15 (C4 to D5): The *A* has reversed itself. No. 16 (C5 to D5): The squares have exchanged places. No. 17 (D2 to E2): Who's that hiding behind the cab? May the force be with him. No. 18 (D3 to E3): This umbrella is so light, it can float in the air. No. 19 (D4): And now it can also keep two people dry at once. No. 20 (E2): That's one expensive cab fare. No. 21 (E5): Did you ever get the feeling that someone was watching you?

The Ultimate Master of Mystery

A final offering from the genius of 221b Baker Street

14
changes

KEEP
SCORE

4min 45sec

A
—
B
—
C
—
D
—
E

1 | 2 | 3 | 4 | 5

Solve this and become a master of mysteries.

ANSWERS No. 1 (A4 to A5): Holmes uses the tube over there to brew coffee. **No. 2** (B3 to C3): Did he create this pigeon through chemistry? **Nos. 3 and 4** (B4 to C4): The lit lamp is donning a smaller shade. **No. 5** (C2): Holmes has developed restless thumb syndrome. **No. 6** (C3): He's lost his blue stick. **No. 7** (D4): A longer valve makes the lamp easier to turn on now. **No. 8** (D5): The flask may be at risk of bubbling over. **No. 9** (D5 to E4): This must be Holmes's violin. **Nos. 10 and 11** (E2): The gold chain has slipped inside his jacket, and he's placed his favorite pipe on the table. **Nos. 12 and 13** (E3): The new pestle is longer, while the glass has been converted into a fog machine. **No. 14** (E4): I wouldn't drink this new blue concoction if I were you.